The Authority Advantage

*Build Your Influence, Impact, and Income
by Sharing What You Know*

Meek Dual

Copyright © 2024 Meek Dual

All rights reserved.

ISBN: 9798343911893

DEDICATION

To and for Pookie.

CONTENTS

PREFACE: *How to Get The Most From This Book*...............1

   Why I Wrote This Book..1

   How to Get the Most from This Book..............................2

   What You'll Learn 4

   You're Ready to Amplify Your Authority 4

INTRODUCTION: *Turning Expertise Into Influence* 6

CHAPTER 1: *The Power of Becoming a Go-To Expert* 9

   What Is Authority, Really?..10

   Why Positioning Yourself as an Expert Matters 11

   The Long-Term Benefits of Being Recognized as an Expert 11

   Your Journey to Authority Starts Here 12

CHAPTER 2: *Finding Your Zone of Genius* 14

   What Is Your Zone of Genius? 15

   Why Identifying Your Zone of Genius Is Key to Becoming an Authority..16

   Finding Your Own Zone of Genius 16

   Moving Forward with Clarity 18

CHAPTER 3: *Storytelling as Your Superpower* 20

Why Storytelling Is Key to Building Authority...............21

Crafting Your Own Story to Build Authority 22

Using Storytelling to Build Your Authority....................25

CHAPTER 4: *Building a Personal Brand That Resonates*...27

Why Your Personal Brand Matters 28

Actionable Steps for Building a Personal Brand That Resonates 28

Moving Forward: Aligning Your Brand with Your Authority 32

CHAPTER 5: *Packaging Your Expertise Into Products and Services* 34

Why Packaging Your Expertise Is Essential for Growth 35

How to Package Your Expertise into Marketable Products and Services..36

Elevating Your Authority and Creating New Revenue Streams..39

CHAPTER 6: *Building and Engaging Your Community* 41

Why Building a Community Elevates Your Authority ...42

How to Build and Engage a Community Around Your Expertise 43

The Long-Term Benefits of Building a Community 46

CHAPTER 7: *Mastering Public Speaking and Presenting* ..49

Why Public Speaking Elevates Your Authority 50

How to Secure Speaking Engagements and Present with Confidence 51

Public Speaking as a Pathway to Authority 54

CHAPTER 8: *Leveraging Content Creation to Build Authority* 57

Why Content Creation is Key to Staying Relevant and Building Authority 58

Building a Sustainable Content Creation Strategy 59

The Long-Term Impact of Consistent Content Creation 62

CHAPTER 9: *Evolving as an Expert—Staying Relevant in a Changing World* 64

Why Ongoing Learning is Crucial for Maintaining Authority 65

Strategies for Staying Relevant in Your Field 66

The Long-Term Benefits of Continuous Learning 69

CHAPTER 10: Monetizing Your Authority for Long-Term Success 71

Why Monetizing Your Authority Is Essential for Long-Term Success 72

Blueprint for Turning Your Authority into a Profitable Business 73

Long-Term Success Through Diversification 76

CONCLUSION: *Creating Your Legacy of Expertise* 78

Anyone Can Become an Authority 79

Take the First Steps Toward Your Authority.................79

Believe in Your Impact..80

BOOKS IN THIS SERIES: *The Course Creator's Toolkit*.......82

Book 1: The Authority Advantage: Build Your Influence, Impact, and Income by Sharing What You Know 83

Book 2: Course Creator's Gold: Build Interactive Courses that Stick and SELL..84

Book 3: Followers to Friends: Build Authentic Connections and Lasting Success Online 86

ABOUT THE AUTHOR 88

ACKNOWLEDGMENTS

First and foremost, I want to thank my mother, **Dorothy Banks**, for giving me the literal space to write—both the physical room to create and the emotional room to grow. Mom, your unwavering belief in me has been my foundation. You've always made space for my dreams, and for that, I'm forever grateful.

To my best friend and soul sister, **Feliciann Malloy**—there aren't enough words to express my gratitude. You've been my biggest cheerleader and my sounding board, helping me navigate the ups and downs of business and life with grace and laughter. Thank you for always having my back, for the late-night brainstorming sessions, and for your endless encouragement. This journey would have been a lot harder—and a lot less fun—without you by my side.

To my incredible **clients**, thank you for your patience and trust as I refined my system and figured out how best to serve you. Your willingness to go along on this ride with me has been a gift. Each of you played a role in shaping this book and the process behind it, and I couldn't have done it without you. Your success stories continue to inspire me every day.

To everyone who has supported me, cheered for me, or just believed in me—this book is as much yours as it is mine. Thank you, from the bottom of my heart, for being part of my journey.

.

PREFACE:
How to Get The Most From This Book

Welcome to *The Authority Advantage*. If you're here, it's because you already possess something incredibly valuable—your knowledge. Whether you're an entrepreneur, coach, consultant, or creative professional, you've likely accumulated a wealth of experience, expertise, and insights. But knowing something is just the beginning. The true transformation happens when you learn how to **share what you know** in a way that builds **influence**, creates **impact**, and generates **income**. This book is your roadmap for doing just that.

Why I Wrote This Book

I've spent years helping professionals, like you, turn their expertise into thriving businesses by learning how to package, share, and monetize what they know. Over time, I noticed a common theme: many incredibly talented people struggle with positioning themselves as the *go-to* experts in their fields. They have the skills, but they don't know how to leverage them to build authority.

That's why I wrote *The Authority Advantage*. My goal is to help you unlock the power of your expertise by showing you how to **build authority** in your niche, **connect** with your audience, and **scale your impact**. This isn't just about achieving professional success; it's about leaving a lasting legacy by sharing what you know in a way that resonates with others.

How to Get the Most from This Book

To help you succeed, I've structured the book in a way that gives you clear, actionable steps to follow. Each chapter builds on the last, guiding you through the process of positioning yourself as an authority, creating a powerful personal brand, and developing products and services that leverage your expertise. Here's how to make sure you're getting the most out of every chapter:

1. **Read with Intent**
   As you move through each chapter, take the time to think about how the concepts apply to your own situation. Whether it's identifying your zone of genius, crafting your personal brand, or packaging your expertise into products, reflect on how you can personalize the strategies to suit your field. Don't rush—let each concept sink in and consider how it aligns with your goals.

2. **Take Action**
   This book is packed with practical exercises and actionable advice. The key to unlocking your authority is to **implement** what you learn. I encourage you to pause at the end of each chapter

and complete the exercises. These aren't just theoretical ideas—they are the same strategies I've used with my clients to help them build their influence, impact, and income. The more you engage with the exercises, the more you'll start to see results.

3. **Use It as a Reference Guide**
   The Authority Advantage isn't just meant to be read once and set aside. Think of it as a resource you can return to throughout your journey. As you grow, revisit specific sections to refine your approach, whether you're looking to update your brand, create new products, or deepen your connection with your audience.

4. **Track Your Progress**
   Building authority takes time, and it's important to track your progress along the way. As you apply the concepts in this book, take note of what's working for you—whether it's increased engagement, new clients, or more opportunities for collaboration. Celebrate those wins! By tracking your journey, you'll be able to see how far you've come and make adjustments as needed.

5. **Stay Open to Evolving**
   Becoming a go-to expert is a journey, not a destination. You'll learn and grow as you implement these strategies, and you'll need to evolve as your industry and audience change. Stay flexible and open to adjusting your approach as you continue to build your influence. Authority is dynamic, and the more you evolve, the more you'll stay ahead of the curve.

What You'll Learn

In this book, you'll discover how to:

- **Find Your Zone of Genius:** Identify the unique strengths and skills that set you apart in your field.

- **Build a Personal Brand:** Craft a brand that resonates with your ideal audience and showcases your expertise.

- **Package Your Expertise:** Turn your knowledge into profitable products and services, from online courses to premium coaching.

- **Engage Your Audience:** Create content that builds trust, drives engagement, and amplifies your authority.

- **Stay Relevant:** Evolve and adapt to industry changes while continuing to grow your influence.

- **Monetize Your Authority:** Learn how to build multiple income streams by leveraging your expertise.

You're Ready to Amplify Your Authority

As you begin this journey, know that you already have everything you need to succeed. Your expertise is valuable, and this book will help you turn it into something that creates lasting influence, impact, and income. My hope is that by the end of *The Authority Advantage*, you will not only see yourself as an expert but also understand how to amplify that authority to achieve your biggest goals.

Now it's time to take action. Let's dive in and start

building your **authority advantage**.

— Meek Dual

INTRODUCTION:
Turning Expertise Into Influence

I didn't set out to become an authority in my field; in fact, for a long time, I wasn't even sure how to channel my skills into something tangible. As a single mother of children, two on the autism spectrum, I was often juggling multiple roles just to keep the lights on. Between being a mom, a project manager, a designer, and a trainer, life was chaotic. But those very struggles became the foundation for what I now call "Meek's Magic"—a unique blend of storytelling, design, and leadership that helped me turn my expertise into influence.

It wasn't an easy road. Like many professionals, I felt stuck and overwhelmed. I had all these skills but wasn't sure how to package them into something that would make me stand out. I knew I had value to offer, but figuring out how to present it, how to get others to recognize it, was the challenge. And I wasn't alone in feeling that way.

Maybe you can relate. Perhaps you're a skilled professional with years of experience, but no one really sees you as the expert you know you are. You're overwhelmed, unsure how to turn your knowledge into something meaningful—something that not only serves others but also elevates your career and financial freedom. The frustration of feeling unseen and undervalued is all too real, and it can make even the most passionate person question their abilities.

But here's the thing: **you already have what it takes** to become a go-to expert in your field. It's not about adding more to your plate or reinventing yourself; it's about packaging your expertise in a way that commands attention. Authority isn't about being the loudest in the room—it's about being the most trusted. And once you position yourself as the expert others rely on, it will unlock new levels of success, confidence, and even financial security that you didn't think possible.

In this book, I'm going to show you how to do exactly that. Whether you're a seasoned professional or someone who's just starting to think about how to elevate your personal brand, you'll learn the steps to package your unique skills, market your expertise, and become the trusted go-to expert in your industry.

I've spent years refining my skills, and along the way, I've mastered the art of leading cross-functional teams, building engaging learning experiences, and crafting compelling narratives that stick. From designing large-scale government initiatives to leading AI and data science projects, my experience in project management, instructional design, and content creation has given me the tools to help others unlock their potential. I've walked the path, and now, I'm here to guide you through it.

By the end of this book, you'll have a solid framework for turning your knowledge into influence. You'll know how to identify your niche, build a personal brand that resonates, and position yourself as the authority others turn to for solutions. And, most importantly, you'll feel confident and equipped to take control of your career.

So, are you ready to step into your role as an authority in your field? Let's begin the journey together.

Now that you understand the power of expertise and how becoming an authority can unlock new levels of success, it's time to dive deeper into what that transformation actually looks like. Throughout this book, you'll hear stories of individuals who, just like you, were once unsure of how to package their skills into something that others would recognize as valuable. One by one, these professionals learned how to position themselves as the go-to experts in their fields, and it changed everything—from their career trajectory to their financial stability.

Let's start with one such story.

CHAPTER 1:
The Power of Becoming a Go-To Expert

When I first started working with Sarah, she was a skilled nutritionist, passionate about helping people lead healthier lives. But despite her expertise and years of experience, she struggled to make a lasting impact. Her clients appreciated her advice, but she wasn't attracting new clients, nor was she recognized as the go-to expert she knew she could be. She felt invisible in a crowded market of health coaches and nutritionists, unsure how to stand out from the competition.

Sarah reached out to me for guidance, and together, we set out to transform her approach. The first thing we tackled was her **positioning**. She wasn't just a nutritionist—she was an expert in sustainable nutrition for busy professionals, people who often found it difficult to balance their work lives with their health. We helped her refine her messaging and personal brand to speak directly to this audience, highlighting her unique approach to meal planning and healthy living in a way that resonated with their pain points.

Next, Sarah began to share her knowledge more strategically. We worked on a content plan that positioned her as a thought leader in her niche—regular blog posts, webinars, and even a mini online course tailored to her audience's specific needs. As she consistently delivered valuable content, people started to notice. They saw her as someone who understood their struggles and could provide actionable solutions. Over time, Sarah didn't have to chase clients—they came to her. Her reputation as an expert grew, her client base expanded, and her income tripled within a year.

But more than that, Sarah's confidence in herself skyrocketed. She no longer felt like one of many. She was **the** go-to nutritionist for professionals who needed a sustainable, realistic approach to healthy eating. She had become an authority in her field.

What Is Authority, Really?

Authority isn't just about having knowledge—it's about positioning yourself as the trusted source people turn to when they need answers or solutions. In Sarah's case, it wasn't enough for her to know a lot about nutrition. To truly stand out, she needed to be seen as the expert who could provide real solutions to her target audience's specific problems.

Think about the experts you follow in your own life. Whether it's a business leader, a fitness coach, or a thought leader in your industry, what draws you to them? More often than not, it's because you trust their judgment and believe they have the answers to your challenges. That's what authority looks like. It's not just about being knowledgeable—it's about being **trusted** to provide insight and guidance in a way that's valuable and actionable for others.

Why Positioning Yourself as an Expert Matters

When you become a recognized authority in your field, everything changes. First, it shifts how people perceive you. Rather than seeing you as just another professional, they begin to view you as the solution to their problem. This shift leads to more opportunities—whether it's attracting new clients, speaking engagements, or media features. People actively seek you out because they want to tap into your expertise.

But the benefits go beyond just professional recognition. Becoming an authority can also transform your self-confidence. Like Sarah, you begin to see yourself not just as someone with knowledge, but as someone whose insights make a difference in other people's lives. And that confidence translates into your work, your relationships, and your ability to continue growing your influence.

The Long-Term Benefits of Being Recognized as an Expert

Positioning yourself as an authority has a ripple effect that extends far beyond the immediate gains of recognition. Over time, it allows you to:

1. **Build a Loyal Audience:** People will begin to follow your work because they trust your expertise. This audience becomes a powerful asset—whether you're launching a new product, marketing a course,

or sharing new content, they are more likely to engage because they see you as a credible source.

2. **Attract Higher-Value Opportunities:** As your reputation grows, so do the opportunities that come your way. Higher-profile clients, speaking engagements, media appearances, and partnerships are just a few of the doors that open when you're known as an authority.

3. **Create Financial Freedom:** When people see you as the go-to expert, they are willing to pay a premium for your services. Whether you're offering coaching, consulting, or products, being an authority allows you to charge what you're worth, without constantly having to justify your prices.

4. **Shape the Conversation in Your Industry:** As an authority, you have the power to influence your industry's direction. You're not just a participant in the conversation—you're leading it. You can set trends, introduce new ideas, and impact how others think and work in your field.

Your Journey to Authority Starts Here

The good news is that the process of becoming a go-to expert is **learnable**. Just like Sarah, you can take deliberate steps to position yourself as the trusted authority in your industry. It's not about being the loudest or most famous. It's about being consistent, credible, and focused on delivering real value.

In the next chapters, I'm going to walk you through the exact steps to get there. You'll learn how to identify your unique strengths, build a personal brand that resonates with your audience, and create the kinds of products and content that establish you as the expert people turn to for guidance.

But first, ask yourself: What would it mean for your career or business if you became the go-to expert in your field? How would it change the way you work, the clients you attract, or the impact you make?

Whatever your answer is, I'm here to help you get there.

Key Takeaway: Authority isn't just about what you know—it's about how you position yourself as the trusted expert people turn to for solutions. Becoming a go-to expert opens doors to new opportunities, financial freedom, and long-term success.

Now that you understand the power and long-term benefits of becoming an authority, you might be asking yourself: How do I actually begin this journey? How do I set myself apart from the countless others who have knowledge in my field? It all starts with discovering your **zone of genius**—the unique intersection of your skills, passions, and market needs that only you can offer. Once you tap into that, your path to authority becomes much clearer. Let me share how I found mine, and then I'll help you uncover yours..

CHAPTER 2:
Finding Your Zone of Genius

My journey to becoming an authority didn't happen overnight. For years, I wore many hats—project manager, instructional designer, graphic artist, storyteller—each role serving its purpose but none of them fully capturing the value I had to offer. I was skilled at designing courses, crafting engaging content, and leading teams, but it wasn't until I found the **intersection** of these talents that things truly clicked.

I call this intersection my **zone of genius**.

For me, the turning point came when I realized I wasn't just a course creator or just a storyteller—I was someone who could **weave the two together** to help others turn their knowledge into transformative learning experiences. I could see the bigger picture, from concept to creation, and help others take their ideas and package them in ways that had a lasting impact. That realization changed everything.

Once I understood my zone of genius, my career

transformed. I wasn't just delivering services; I was providing **high-impact solutions** that resonated deeply with my clients. I became the go-to person for course creation strategies that combined powerful narratives with instructional design. My expertise became about more than just the tasks I could perform—it became about the **value I could create** by using my unique blend of skills to solve problems for others.

What Is Your Zone of Genius?

Your zone of genius is the unique combination of skills, experiences, and passions that only **you** can bring to the table. It's the space where you excel naturally and where your talents align with something the world truly needs. When you're operating in your zone of genius, work feels more like flow—it's challenging but rewarding, and it taps into your true strengths.

But here's the thing: most people spend their time in their **zone of competence** or **zone of excellence** rather than their zone of genius.

- **Zone of Competence**: This is where you're doing tasks that you're capable of, but they don't inspire or energize you. These are things you can do well but aren't particularly unique to you.

- **Zone of Excellence**: Here, you're doing work that you're great at, tasks that you're known for and can perform better than most. But even in this zone, there's still a feeling of "something more"—like you're not tapping into your full potential.

Your **zone of genius** is where everything comes together—your passion, your natural talents, and your ability to serve others. It's the work that not only makes a difference but also feels fulfilling and deeply aligned with who you are.

Why Identifying Your Zone of Genius Is Key to Becoming an Authority

If you're serious about becoming an authority in your field, you can't just be good at what you do—you need to **own** the unique value that only you can offer. When you operate from your zone of genius, you create something that's hard to replicate. It's this uniqueness that will set you apart from everyone else and help you stand out as the trusted expert people turn to.

Once you identify your zone of genius, everything becomes clearer. You'll know where to focus your time and energy, and you'll naturally attract the right opportunities because you're delivering value that aligns perfectly with what the market needs.

Finding Your Own Zone of Genius

So, how do you find your zone of genius? Let's walk through a few exercises that will help you identify your unique strengths and passions, and figure out how to align those with market needs.

1. The Genius Reflection Exercise

Start by reflecting on your past experiences and asking yourself the following questions:

- What activities make me feel energized and fulfilled?

- When do I feel like I'm truly in my element?
- What tasks do I do that others consistently praise me for?
- What kinds of challenges do I enjoy solving the most?
- When have I experienced moments of "flow," where time seems to fly because I'm so immersed in what I'm doing?

As you answer these questions, notice any patterns or recurring themes. These are clues to your zone of genius.

2. Identify Your Superpowers

Think about the one or two things that **only you** can do better than anyone else. It's tempting to dismiss our strengths because they come so naturally to us, but your superpowers often live in the skills you find effortless but others find difficult. Ask friends, colleagues, or clients for their input on this. What do they see as your greatest strengths?

For example, in my case, it was the ability to **tell stories** that not only engaged people but also turned complex ideas into actionable strategies. It wasn't something I thought of as a "superpower" until I realized how valuable that combination of skills was for my clients.

3. Find the Intersection Between Your Passion and Market Needs

Your zone of genius isn't just about what you love doing; it's also about what **the world needs**. This is where many people get stuck—they focus only on their passions but don't consider whether those passions solve a real problem for others. To become a go-to expert, you need to align your genius with a need that exists in the marketplace.

Ask yourself:

- What problems am I uniquely qualified to solve?
- Who is my ideal audience, and what are they struggling with?
- How can I use my unique strengths to create solutions that resonate with them?

4. Craft Your Genius Statement

Once you've reflected on these questions, it's time to articulate your zone of genius in a way that's clear and compelling. Write a statement that sums up what you do, who you serve, and what makes you uniquely qualified to help them.

For example, my genius statement could be: *"I help professionals and entrepreneurs package their expertise into high-impact learning experiences by combining storytelling, course design, and strategic vision, so they can grow their influence and achieve lasting success."*

Your genius statement should feel like a natural extension of who you are and the value you bring to the table. It will become a cornerstone of how you position yourself as an authority in your field.

Moving Forward with Clarity

Finding your zone of genius is a game-changer. Once you

identify it, you'll stop wasting energy on tasks that don't serve your purpose and instead focus on what truly sets you apart. Operating from this space will not only boost your confidence but will also allow you to create greater impact and influence in your industry.

As we move into the next chapter, you'll learn how to take your zone of genius and **build a personal brand** around it that resonates with your audience. With this clarity, you'll be able to confidently position yourself as the go-to expert in your field.

Key Takeaway: Your zone of genius is the intersection of your natural talents, passions, and the market's needs. By identifying this space, you'll unlock the key to positioning yourself as an authority in your field and create a unique value proposition that sets you apart from the competition.

Now that you've discovered your zone of genius—the unique intersection of your talents, passions, and market needs—it's time to bring it to life. The most powerful tool you have to showcase your expertise and connect with your audience is storytelling. It's one thing to know what sets you apart; it's another to communicate that in a way that resonates deeply with others. In this next chapter, we'll explore how storytelling can transform your brand and position you as the go-to expert in your field.

CHAPTER 3:
Storytelling as Your Superpower

When I first started building my personal brand, I knew I had a blend of skills that made me valuable—storytelling, instructional design, and the ability to translate complex ideas into simple, actionable steps. But the real turning point came when I realized that **storytelling** wasn't just one of my skills; it was the *cornerstone* of everything I did.

I remember the moment clearly. I was designing an online course for a client who struggled with low engagement. They had all the right information but couldn't connect with their audience. I sat down with them, and we began reshaping their course content, not around facts and data, but around stories. We started with why they cared about the subject in the first place, weaving in personal anecdotes and real-life examples. By the time we finished, the course wasn't just informative—it was **compelling**.

The result? Not only did engagement soar, but the course participants began seeing real results because the content resonated with them on a deeper level. It wasn't just about learning new information—it was about connecting with a narrative that spoke to their own struggles and aspirations. This project was a turning point for me as well. I realized that storytelling was more than just a tool—it was the *bridge* between my expertise and the impact I wanted to make.

Storytelling became the foundation of my brand. Whether I was designing a course, writing content, or coaching others, the stories I shared created trust, authenticity, and emotional connections. My audience wasn't just listening to information; they were engaging with my journey and my experiences, which made my advice more relatable and actionable.

Why Storytelling Is Key to Building Authority

To become an authority in your field, you need more than just facts and figures. People don't connect with data; they connect with **stories**. Stories create an emotional bond between you and your audience, building trust and making your message memorable.

Think about the experts you follow. Chances are, they've shared personal stories that resonated with you—moments of struggle, breakthrough, or success. Those stories gave you insight not just into what they know, but who they are. That's the power of storytelling. It humanizes your expertise, making it more relatable and trustworthy.

When you tell your story, you're not just sharing information; you're showing your audience:

- **Why they should trust you** (because you've been where they are),

- **How you've used your expertise** to solve real problems,
- **What makes you unique** compared to others in your field.

Authority isn't just about being knowledgeable. It's about being trusted. And trust is built through vulnerability, authenticity, and relatability—qualities that are best communicated through storytelling.

Crafting Your Own Story to Build Authority

So, how do you tell your story in a way that positions you as an expert and builds trust with your audience? Let's walk through a framework that will help you craft a powerful narrative around your expertise:

1. Start with Your "Why"

Every great story starts with a purpose. Why do you do what you do? What inspired you to get into your field in the first place? Your "why" is the driving force behind your passion and expertise, and it's what makes you relatable to your audience.

For me, my "why" was shaped by the challenges I faced as a single mother, balancing multiple roles and finding ways to package my expertise into something meaningful. That personal story became the backbone of my brand because it showed that I wasn't just someone with skills—I was someone who understood struggle, resilience, and the journey to success.

Exercise: Write down the moment or experience that inspired you to pursue your career or expertise. Why is this work important to you? How does your personal journey align with the work you do today?

2. Highlight a Struggle or Challenge

Every compelling story involves overcoming a challenge. Sharing your struggles doesn't make you weak—it makes you **human**. When you're open about the obstacles you've faced, it allows your audience to see themselves in your journey. They connect with your vulnerability, and that connection builds trust.

In my case, I often share the story of how I had to juggle different roles, unsure of how to turn my scattered talents into something cohesive. That challenge is something many of my clients relate to, and it's what makes them trust my advice. They know I've been through similar struggles and found a way forward.

Exercise: Think of a time when you faced a significant challenge in your career or personal life. How did you overcome it? How did it shape the way you approach your work today? Write down the details of that experience and how it made you stronger or more insightful.

3. Share Your Transformation

After the struggle comes the breakthrough. What did you learn from your challenges? How did you grow or evolve? This transformation is what positions you as an expert. You're not just telling a story of struggle; you're showing how you gained the knowledge and expertise to help others.

In my storytelling, I emphasize how I discovered my zone of genius—how I learned to package my storytelling, instructional design, and content creation into a unified offering that helped others. That transformation shows my audience that I'm not just teaching theories—I'm sharing what I've *lived*.

Exercise: Write down the turning point in your story. What was the moment when things started to shift for you? How did you gain the knowledge or skills that now define your expertise?

4. Connect Your Story to Your Audience's Needs

A great story is not just about you—it's about your audience. The goal is to show them that your journey can help them overcome their own challenges. How does your story relate to the problems your audience is facing? What can they learn from your experience that will help them succeed?

For example, when I share my story of finding my zone of genius, it's not just to talk about myself—it's to help my audience realize that they, too, have unique talents that can be packaged into something powerful. My story becomes a guidepost for their journey.

Exercise: Think about your ideal audience. What are their biggest struggles or challenges? How can your personal story offer them a solution or insight? Write down the ways your journey connects to their needs and aspirations.

5. End with a Call to Action

Finally, every good story leaves the audience with a next step. What do you want your audience to do after hearing your story? Do you want them to reflect on their own journey? Do you want them to take action by working with you or applying what they've learned? Make your call to action clear and specific.

In my case, I often end my storytelling with a call to action, inviting my audience to take the first step in their own transformation—whether that's enrolling in a course, joining a coaching program, or simply reflecting on their own strengths.

Exercise: Write a simple call to action that encourages your audience to take the next step toward their own growth. Whether it's something small like journaling about their own journey or reaching out to work with you, make it actionable.

Using Storytelling to Build Your Authority

By weaving your personal story into your brand, you create a narrative that not only highlights your expertise but also makes it deeply relatable and trustworthy. When your audience sees your vulnerability, your struggles, and your growth, they're more likely to trust you and see you as someone who can guide them through their own challenges.

As you move forward, remember that storytelling isn't a one-time event—it's an ongoing practice. Share your stories across your content, whether in blog posts, social media, videos, or courses. The more you tell your story, the stronger your connection with your audience will become, and the more your authority will grow.

Key Takeaway: Crafting a compelling narrative around your expertise is essential to building trust and positioning yourself as an authority. By sharing your "why," your struggles, and your transformation, you create a story that resonates with your audience and makes your expertise relatable, trustworthy, and actionable.

Now that you've seen the power of storytelling and how it connects you with your audience, it's time to take the next critical step: building a personal brand that reflects your unique story and expertise. Your brand is how people experience you—it's how they identify and connect with the value you offer. In the next chapter, we'll explore how to create a brand that not only resonates with your audience but also solidifies your position as an authority in your field. Let me share how I crafted "Meek's Magic" and how it transformed my own journey.

CHAPTER 4:
Building a Personal Brand That Resonates

When I first set out to establish myself as an authority, I knew I needed something that set me apart—something that captured not only what I did but also **who I was**. That's when "Meek's Magic" was born. It wasn't just a catchy phrase; it was the essence of what I brought to every project—this unique blend of creativity, storytelling, and instructional design that could transform ideas into experiences.

At the heart of "Meek's Magic" was my belief that real impact comes from creating deep connections—whether through a beautifully designed course, an engaging presentation, or a coaching session that inspires real change. But more than that, my brand was about the **experience** my clients had when working with me: feeling supported, encouraged, and empowered.

As I built this brand, something amazing happened. My audience began to see me not just as someone who provided services, but as someone they could trust to help them navigate their challenges and reach their goals. My brand didn't just make me visible—it created **connection**. And that's the secret to building a brand that resonates: it's not about standing out in a crowded market just to be noticed; it's about standing out because you connect deeply with the people you're meant to serve.

Why Your Personal Brand Matters

A strong, authentic personal brand is the foundation of becoming a go-to expert. In a world full of noise, your brand is what helps people recognize you, trust you, and ultimately choose you. But it's not just about having a catchy logo or a polished social media presence—it's about being **consistent and authentic** in how you show up.

When you create a brand that's true to your values and aligned with your expertise, you build trust with your audience. And trust is the currency of authority. People don't follow or hire you just because you know what you're doing—they choose you because they **believe** in your story, your approach, and your ability to help them.

Your personal brand is what makes you memorable. It's what helps you stand out in a crowded field of experts and ensures that people think of you when they need solutions. Most importantly, it's about creating a sense of connection with your audience so that they feel drawn to your message and your services.

Actionable Steps for Building a Personal Brand That Resonates

So how do you go about building a personal brand that truly

resonates with your audience and sets you up as the expert they turn to? Let's break it down into actionable steps:

1. Define Your Brand's Core Values

Your personal brand starts with understanding your **core values**—the principles that guide your work and how you interact with others. These values should reflect what matters most to you and how you want to show up in the world. When your brand aligns with your values, it feels authentic, and people can sense that authenticity.

For me, "Meek's Magic" was built on values like **creativity**, **support**, and **empowerment**. Everything I do is grounded in helping others unlock their potential in creative, impactful ways. These values guide how I engage with my clients, how I approach my work, and how I communicate my message.

Exercise: Write down the top three values that are central to who you are and how you want to run your business or career. How do these values show up in your work? Make sure these values become the foundation of your brand.

2. Identify Your Brand's Unique Promise

Every personal brand needs a **promise**—a clear message about what your audience can expect from you. This promise should be rooted in your zone of genius and what you can uniquely offer. It's not about promising to be everything to everyone; it's about promising to deliver **consistent, specific value** to your target audience.

For example, my brand promise is simple: I help people package their expertise into high-impact learning experiences that inspire and drive change. I don't promise to do everything related to instructional design or content creation, but I do promise to deliver experiences that captivate and resonate.

Exercise: Write a clear brand promise. What is the one thing your audience can consistently count on you for? Make it specific, and let it speak to your strengths and expertise.

3. Define Your Ideal Audience

To build a brand that resonates, you need to be crystal clear about who you're trying to connect with. Your brand isn't for everyone, and that's a good thing. The more you can tailor your brand to your **ideal audience**, the more deeply you'll connect with the right people—the ones who need what you have to offer.

For "Meek's Magic," I've always been focused on serving entrepreneurs, creatives, and professionals who want to turn their expertise into something meaningful—whether through courses, content, or personal branding. These are people who value creativity and are ready to do the work to unlock their potential. Knowing this helps me tailor everything I do, from my messaging to my services, to fit their specific needs.

Exercise: Describe your ideal audience. Who are they? What are their challenges, and how does your brand solve them? The more specific you can be, the better.

4. Craft Your Brand's Visual and Verbal Identity

Your brand's **visual and verbal identity**—the way it looks and sounds—is how people will experience your brand across different platforms. This includes your logo, colors, fonts, tone of voice, and the way you

communicate in written and spoken formats. The goal is to ensure that all of these elements align with your core values, brand promise, and audience's needs.

For example, with "Meek's Magic," my brand visuals are designed to evoke creativity and empowerment. The colors are vibrant yet professional, reflecting both the innovative and supportive nature of my services. My tone of voice, whether in blog posts, social media, or client communications, is encouraging and straightforward, reflecting my commitment to helping others succeed.

It's important to create consistency across all your platforms, so whether someone reads your blog, visits your website, or attends your webinar, they immediately recognize your brand. Consistency builds trust, and trust builds authority.

Exercise: Create a mood board that reflects your brand's look and feel. Choose colors, fonts, and images that align with the values you want to convey. Then, write down a few key phrases that capture the tone and voice of your brand. Is it formal, conversational, empowering, or informative?

5. Tell Your Brand's Story

Your personal brand should always be grounded in a story—**your story**. As we discussed in the previous chapter, storytelling is the key to connecting with your audience on a deeper level. This is where you share your journey, the challenges you've faced, and how those experiences have shaped the expert you are today.

For me, the "Meek's Magic" brand story is rooted in my experiences as a single mother who juggled multiple roles and found a way to package her talents into something meaningful. It's this story of perseverance and creativity that resonates with my audience because many of them are navigating similar challenges.

Exercise: Write the narrative of your brand. Start with your "why"—what brought you into this field? What challenges did you overcome? How did you discover your zone of genius? Make sure this story is woven into your messaging, from your website's "About" page to the content you share on social media.

6. Stay Consistent and Evolve Over Time

Finally, building a brand that resonates requires **consistency**. You need to show up regularly, delivering on your brand promise and reinforcing your values through everything you do. But while consistency is key, it's also important to allow your brand to **evolve** as you grow.

Your brand may change as you refine your expertise, expand your services, or adapt to new market needs. The important thing is to stay true to your core values and continue building meaningful connections with your audience.

Exercise: Set up a system for regularly evaluating your brand. Every few months, review your messaging, visuals, and audience engagement to ensure they still reflect your values and the direction you're heading. Are there areas where you can evolve or improve while maintaining consistency?

Moving Forward: Aligning Your Brand with Your Authority

Your personal brand is a powerful tool for building authority. When it's rooted in authenticity and aligned with your zone of genius, it becomes the foundation for all your interactions and helps you stand out as the go-to expert in your field. Remember, it's not about creating a brand that pleases everyone—it's about creating a brand that speaks directly to the people who need what you have to offer.

As you move forward, keep refining your brand, stay consistent, and make sure everything you do reinforces the trust and connection you've built with your audience. In the next chapter, we'll explore how to take this brand and **package your expertise** into products and services that further establish your authority.

Key Takeaway: Building a personal brand that resonates is about more than just visibility—it's about creating a connection with your audience by staying true to your core values, telling your story, and delivering on your brand promise. A strong, authentic brand not only sets you apart in a crowded market but also positions you as a trusted authority in your field.

Now that you've built a personal brand that resonates with your audience and communicates your expertise, it's time to take things to the next level. Being recognized as an authority is one thing, but to truly elevate your status and create new revenue streams, you need to package your knowledge into products and services that deliver value. This is how you not only grow your influence but also create sustainable income. In this next chapter, I'll show you how one of my clients did just that, and how you can do the same.

CHAPTER 5:
Packaging Your Expertise Into Products and Services

When I first met Jason, he was a marketing consultant with a wealth of knowledge. He had helped numerous small businesses scale through digital marketing strategies, but he was feeling stuck. Despite his expertise, Jason was constantly trading hours for dollars—working with clients one-on-one and feeling limited by the time he had available. He was exhausted and ready for something more scalable.

Jason had a lot to offer, but he didn't know how to **package** his knowledge in a way that would allow him to serve more people without burning out. That's when we decided to transform his expertise into an online course—a way for him to reach a wider audience and establish himself as a true expert in his niche.

We started by identifying his core expertise: helping small businesses grow through paid advertising and social media campaigns. Jason had a system he had developed over the years, and it was time to turn that system into a tangible product. Together, we built a course that walked small business owners through the exact steps to create and manage successful ad campaigns, from initial setup to optimizing for ROI.

The result? Not only did the course generate a significant new revenue stream for Jason, but it also positioned him as a thought leader in his industry. His course became a go-to resource for small businesses, and his consulting business thrived as a result. People no longer saw Jason as just another consultant—they saw him as an **expert** who had created a proven, accessible system for success.

Why Packaging Your Expertise Is Essential for Growth

Like Jason, many experts find themselves in a similar situation—working hard, delivering value to individual clients, but unable to scale their knowledge. The solution? **Packaging** your expertise into products or services that can be delivered to a wider audience, without you having to be directly involved every time.

To truly stand out as an authority in your field, you need to offer more than just one-on-one services. Tangible products—whether it's an online course, a book, a digital product, or a coaching program—allow you to showcase your knowledge, reach more people, and create new streams of income.

Here's why this matters:

- **Scalability:** Once your expertise is packaged into a product, it can be sold repeatedly without requiring your time for every sale.

- **Reach:** With products like courses or books, you can reach a much larger audience than you could ever serve one-on-one.

- **Credibility:** When you create a product that showcases your expertise, it elevates your status as an authority because you're providing structured, accessible solutions.

- **Revenue Diversification:** Packaging your expertise opens up new revenue streams that can bring in consistent income, whether you're working directly with clients or not.

How to Package Your Expertise into Marketable Products and Services

If you want to elevate your authority and grow your income, it's time to start thinking about how to package your expertise into products and services that resonate with your audience. Here's how you can do it:

1. Identify Your Core Expertise and Audience Needs

The first step in packaging your expertise is identifying your **core offering**. What specific knowledge or skills do you have that people would pay for? What do your clients or audience consistently ask for help with? Your product or service should address a clear pain point or need that your target audience faces.

For Jason, his expertise in digital marketing for small businesses was the foundation for his course. We focused on the **exact problem** his audience faced: struggling to set up and optimize ad campaigns on a budget.

Exercise: Write down the top 2-3 areas of expertise you have. Then, list out the most common questions or challenges your audience faces related to those areas. This is where your product or service should focus.

2. Choose the Right Format

There are many ways to package your expertise into something marketable. The key is choosing a format that aligns with both your strengths and your audience's preferences. Here are a few common formats:

- **Online Course:** Perfect for teaching step-by-step processes or sharing in-depth knowledge. This format is scalable and can generate passive income over time.

- **Consulting Packages:** Instead of offering one-off consultations, package your services into a longer-term consulting package with defined deliverables.

- **Books or eBooks:** Ideal for those who prefer writing or have knowledge that can be shared in a structured, digestible format.

- **Membership or Coaching Programs:** These offer ongoing value and access to your expertise, often through group coaching or a subscription-based model.

- **Digital Products:** Templates, workbooks, or guides that help solve specific problems your audience faces.

Jason chose an online course because it allowed him to demonstrate his expertise through video tutorials and practical exercises—something that suited his teaching style and gave his audience hands-on learning.

Exercise: Based on your expertise and how your audience prefers to consume content, brainstorm which format would best suit your product. Consider your strengths—do you enjoy teaching, writing, or creating digital tools? Choose the format that feels most aligned with both your skills and audience needs.

3. Create a Framework or System

Your audience is looking for structure. They want a clear path from where they are now to where they want to be, and that's where your **framework** or **system** comes in. When you package your expertise into a product, it's important to create a step-by-step process that people can follow.

For Jason's course, we broke down his digital marketing expertise into clear, actionable modules: understanding audience targeting, setting up ads, creating compelling content, and optimizing for success. This system allowed his audience to learn at their own pace and see measurable results.

Exercise: Break your expertise down into clear steps, modules, or phases. What process do you use when working with clients? How can you structure that into a system that's easy to follow?

4. Develop and Market Your Product

Once you've chosen your format and created your framework, it's time to develop the actual product. For a course, this might involve recording video lessons and creating workbooks. For a consulting package, it could be outlining your services, deliverables, and pricing. For a book, it's about writing and structuring your content.

After development, marketing becomes crucial. You need to **position** your product in front of your audience. Utilize your personal brand, your storytelling skills, and your content platforms to market your expertise in a way that resonates with your target audience. Leverage social media, email marketing, webinars, and collaborations to spread the word.

Jason launched his course through a series of live webinars, offering sneak peeks of the content and demonstrating the value it provided. This not only built excitement but also established trust with potential buyers.

Exercise: Create a simple marketing plan for your product. How will you promote it? What channels will you use to reach your audience? Consider running a webinar, creating social media campaigns, or offering early-bird pricing to generate interest.

Elevating Your Authority and Creating New Revenue Streams

By packaging your expertise into products or services, you're not only creating new income streams but also solidifying your authority in your field. People will see you as more than just someone with knowledge—they'll see you as someone who offers **tangible solutions**. This positions you as the expert who can deliver real, actionable value.

As you move forward, remember that packaging your expertise is a powerful way to scale your impact and increase your visibility. In the next chapter, we'll dive into how to market your products effectively and grow your audience so that your authority continues to expand.

Key Takeaway: Packaging your expertise into marketable products and services allows you to reach a wider audience, create new revenue streams, and position yourself as a go-to authority. Whether it's a course, book, or consulting package, offering tangible solutions that solve real problems is the key to elevating your influence and growing your business.

Now that you've learned how to package your expertise into products and services, you're ready to expand your reach. But to truly amplify your authority, you need more than just a product—you need a **community**. Building a community of engaged learners or followers not only strengthens your influence but also creates a loyal base of advocates who will champion your work and spread your message. In the next chapter, I'll show you how fostering a community transformed my group coaching program and how you can build one that solidifies your status as an expert.

CHAPTER 6:
Building and Engaging Your Community

When I launched my group coaching program, I wasn't sure what to expect. I knew I had valuable content to offer, but I quickly realized that the true power of the program wasn't just in the lessons I taught—it was in the **community** that formed around it. The participants, who were all at different stages of their journey, began to share their own experiences, support each other, and provide real-time feedback. As the weeks went on, I saw how much they were learning, not just from me, but from **each other**.

By fostering a space where members felt safe to share their challenges and successes, the program became more than just a coaching experience—it became a **community of learners**. That community elevated my authority in ways I hadn't anticipated. The participants began to refer new clients, share testimonials, and even advocate for my work on social media. This wasn't just about me being their coach—it was about **building a network of engaged, supportive individuals** who saw value in both what I offered and what they brought to the table.

Through this experience, I learned a critical lesson: authority doesn't happen in isolation. It's not enough to package your expertise—you have to build a community around it. When people feel connected to you and to each other, they become your advocates, spreading your message far beyond your immediate reach. And the trust and loyalty that develop in a thriving community are what turn casual followers into devoted supporters.

Why Building a Community Elevates Your Authority

A community amplifies your authority by creating a space where people can engage with your expertise on a deeper level. It turns passive consumers into active participants, allowing them to connect not only with you but also with each other. This connection builds **trust** and **loyalty**, both of which are essential to solidifying your status as an expert.

Here's why community is such a powerful tool for growing your authority:

- **Engagement:** A community encourages interaction. The more engaged people are with your content and each other, the more they associate your brand with value and solutions.

- **Trust:** When people connect with others who share their challenges and aspirations, they build trust—not only in the group but in you as the leader.

- **Advocacy:** A loyal community will promote your work, share your content, and refer you to others, amplifying your message far beyond your direct influence.

Authority doesn't grow in isolation. When you create a space where people can come together, share experiences, and learn from one another, you're not just building a following—you're building a **movement** around your expertise.

How to Build and Engage a Community Around Your Expertise

Building a community may seem daunting, but it doesn't have to be complicated. Whether you're creating an online group, leading in-person events, or fostering engagement through social media, the key is to create a space where people feel connected, supported, and encouraged to engage with your expertise and with each other. Here are the steps to building and engaging your own community:

1. Define Your Purpose and Audience

Before you start building a community, it's important to define **why** you're creating it and **who** it's for. What is the primary purpose of your community? Is it to share knowledge, offer support, or create a space for collaboration? And who are the people you want to engage with? The more specific you can be about your community's focus and who it's for, the stronger it will be.

For example, when I started my group coaching program, I knew it was for entrepreneurs and professionals who wanted to package their expertise into online courses. That clarity helped me attract the right people and create content that resonated with their needs.

Exercise: Write down the purpose of your community. What will it provide to your audience that they can't get anywhere else? Who is your ideal community member, and what challenges or goals do they have?

2. Choose the Right Platform

Once you've defined your purpose and audience, it's time to choose the platform where your community will gather. This could be an online forum, a Facebook group, a Slack channel, or even in-person events. The key is to choose a platform that's accessible to your audience and aligns with how they prefer to engage.

For my coaching program, I used a combination of live Zoom sessions and a private Facebook group. The live sessions allowed for real-time interaction, while the Facebook group provided a space for ongoing discussion and support. This blend worked well for my audience, who appreciated both the structured learning and the informal, supportive environment.

Exercise: Think about where your audience is most likely to engage. Are they active on social media? Do they prefer live interaction? Choose a platform that makes it easy for them to participate and engage with your content and each other.

3. Foster Engagement with Valuable Content

A community thrives on engagement, and to spark that engagement, you need to provide **valuable content** that resonates with your members. This doesn't always mean creating new content—it can be about facilitating conversations, asking thought-provoking questions, or encouraging members to share their experiences and insights.

For my group, I made sure to provide regular prompts, share helpful resources, and highlight member success stories. But I also encouraged members to take the lead—asking them to share their own challenges and advice, which helped foster a sense of ownership within the group.

Exercise: Create a content plan for your community. What types of content will you share to keep members engaged? Will you provide educational resources, host Q&A sessions, or highlight community achievements? Make sure your content aligns with the needs and interests of your audience.

4. Encourage Peer-to-Peer Interaction

One of the most powerful aspects of a community is the **peer-to-peer interaction** that happens when members learn from and support each other. While you're the leader of the community, it's important to create space for your members to connect with one another.

In my coaching group, I made it a point to encourage collaboration. Members paired up for accountability, shared resources, and even collaborated on projects. This not only increased engagement but also strengthened the bonds within the community, making it a more dynamic and supportive space.

Exercise: Think about how you can encourage peer-to-peer interaction in your community. Can you set up small group discussions, create accountability pairs, or host collaborative events? The more opportunities you create for members to connect, the stronger your community will become.

5. Nurture Your Community Consistently

Building a community isn't a one-time event—it's an ongoing process that requires **consistent nurturing**. This means regularly engaging with your members, providing fresh content, and responding to their needs. The more you invest in your community, the more it will grow and thrive.

For me, this meant being active in my Facebook group, checking in with members regularly, and making myself available for questions and feedback. I also made sure to celebrate the successes of my community members, which reinforced the positive, supportive culture of the group.

Exercise: Schedule regular check-ins with your community. Whether it's weekly live sessions, monthly Q&A forums, or daily posts, make sure you're consistently engaging with your members and keeping the community active.

The Long-Term Benefits of Building a Community

When you build and engage a community around your expertise, you're not just growing your audience—you're building a loyal network of advocates who will champion your work and elevate your authority. Here's how a thriving community can transform your business and your brand:

- **Increased Trust:** A community provides ongoing interaction with your audience, which builds deeper trust and credibility.

- **Loyalty and Retention:** People who feel connected to you and your community are more likely to stay engaged with your products and services.

- **Word-of-Mouth Growth:** Engaged community members often become your biggest advocates, spreading your message and referring new clients or customers.

- **Feedback and Innovation:** Your community will give you valuable feedback on your content and offerings, helping you improve and innovate over time.

By building a community, you create a space where people feel valued, supported, and connected to your expertise. This is the foundation for long-term growth, both for your personal brand and your business.

As we move into the next chapter, we'll explore how to leverage public speaking and teaching opportunities to further solidify your authority and expand your reach.

Key Takeaway: Building and engaging a community around your expertise is essential for amplifying your authority. By creating a space where your audience can connect with you and each other, you build trust, loyalty, and advocacy, all of which elevate your status as a go-to expert. Consistent engagement, valuable content, and peer-to-peer interaction are the keys to creating a thriving, supportive community.

As your community grows and your authority deepens, there's another powerful tool you can use to take your influence even further—public speaking. Whether it's a live event, a virtual webinar, or a workshop, speaking allows you to showcase your expertise in real time and connect with your audience in ways that other platforms can't match. In the next chapter, we'll explore how mastering public speaking can elevate your authority, and I'll share how one key speaking engagement changed the trajectory of my career.

CHAPTER 7:
Mastering Public Speaking and Presenting

I remember the day clearly. I had been invited to speak at a national conference for entrepreneurs and small business owners, and while I was excited about the opportunity, I also felt the weight of responsibility. This was a room full of experienced professionals, and my session was all about helping them package their expertise into online courses—a topic I knew inside and out, but one that had to be delivered with precision and impact.

As I stood on stage and shared my story—how I had helped others transform their knowledge into powerful, revenue-generating courses—I could feel the room connecting with me. The energy was incredible. People weren't just listening; they were *engaging*, nodding, taking notes, asking questions.

By the end of the session, I had dozens of people lined up, eager to speak with me. Some wanted to work with me one-on-one, while others were interested in joining my upcoming group coaching program. That single speaking engagement led to new clients, partnerships, and even more speaking opportunities.

In that moment, I realized how powerful public speaking can be. It wasn't just about presenting my knowledge—it was about positioning myself as the go-to expert in the room. It built trust instantly and allowed me to connect with people on a deeper level, far beyond what a blog post or social media update could achieve.

Why Public Speaking Elevates Your Authority

Speaking in front of an audience—whether live or virtual—is one of the fastest ways to build authority and showcase your expertise. It allows you to:

- **Demonstrate Your Knowledge:** When you're on stage or leading a workshop, you have the chance to show your depth of understanding in real time. You can share insights, answer questions, and offer tailored advice, which instantly positions you as an expert.

- **Build Trust and Credibility:** People are more likely to trust you when they see you confidently presenting your ideas and solutions in front of an audience. Public speaking showcases not only your expertise but also your ability to communicate effectively and connect with others.

- **Expand Your Reach:** Speaking engagements often lead to new opportunities—whether that's attracting new clients, securing media interviews, or being invited to speak at other events. Each time you speak, you're expanding your network and building your reputation as an authority in your field.

Public speaking isn't just about sharing information; it's about creating **impact**. When done well, it allows you to engage with your audience, offer real value, and leave a lasting impression that elevates your status as a leader in your industry.

How to Secure Speaking Engagements and Present with Confidence

If you want to build your authority through public speaking, the first step is to start **getting in front of audiences**. Whether it's at industry conferences, webinars, or even local workshops, the more you speak, the more confident you'll become—and the more you'll be seen as an expert in your field.

Here's a roadmap to help you get started:

1. Start with Smaller Events or Virtual Platforms

If you're new to public speaking, you don't need to jump into large conferences right away. Start with smaller, more intimate events where you can practice your speaking skills and gain confidence. Virtual platforms like webinars, podcasts, or online workshops are also great for honing your delivery and reaching wider audiences without the pressure of a live stage.

For example, before I spoke at the national conference, I had led several smaller workshops and webinars on course creation. These virtual sessions allowed me to refine my message, test different presentation styles, and get comfortable engaging with an audience.

Exercise: Look for smaller speaking opportunities within your network—local business groups, online communities, or industry-related webinars. Reach out to event organizers or offer to lead a session based on your expertise.

2. Craft a Compelling Presentation

A great presentation isn't just about what you say—it's about **how** you say it. Your presentation should be structured in a way that captures your audience's attention, keeps them engaged, and leaves them with valuable takeaways. Start with a strong hook that draws them in, present your key insights in a clear and organized way, and end with a memorable conclusion or call to action.

When I crafted my talk for the national conference, I focused on telling a story that resonated with the audience. I didn't just list facts or give a dry lecture—I shared personal anecdotes, real-life case studies, and practical steps they could take immediately. This made my presentation both engaging and actionable.

Exercise: Plan your presentation using this simple structure:

- **Introduction/Hook:** Start with a story, question, or surprising fact that grabs attention.

- **Core Message:** Present your main points in a clear, organized way. Use examples and visuals to make your points more relatable.

- **Call to Action:** End with a strong message or action step that motivates your audience to take the next step, whether it's implementing what they've learned or reaching out to work with you.

3. Build Relationships with Event Organizers

One of the best ways to secure speaking engagements is to build relationships with event organizers and decision-makers. These are the people who select speakers for conferences, workshops, and webinars. By connecting with them and showing how your expertise aligns with their event's goals, you increase your chances of being invited to speak.

For me, the opportunity to speak at the national conference came after I had connected with the organizer through a smaller industry event. I made an effort to stay in touch, sharing updates on my work and offering to contribute value to their community. When the opportunity arose, I was already on their radar.

Exercise: Identify events, conferences, or organizations in your industry and reach out to the organizers. Share a brief overview of your expertise and how you can add value to their audience. Offer to present on a topic that aligns with their event's theme or audience needs.

4. Practice and Refine Your Delivery

Even the best content won't land if it's not delivered with confidence and clarity. The key to mastering public speaking is **practice**. The more you rehearse your presentation, the more comfortable and confident you'll feel. Practice in front of a mirror, record yourself, or present to a small group of friends or colleagues.

In my case, I rehearsed my national conference presentation multiple times—refining my timing, adjusting my tone, and even practicing my body language. By the time I got on stage, I knew my material inside and out, which allowed me to focus on connecting with the audience instead of worrying about the details.

Exercise: Practice delivering your presentation in different settings. Record yourself, watch the playback, and look for areas to improve, such as pacing, clarity, or body language. Ask for feedback from peers to ensure your message is landing effectively.

5. Leverage Your Speaking Success for Future Opportunities

Once you've delivered a successful presentation, don't let the momentum stop there. Use that speaking engagement to build future opportunities. Ask for testimonials from event organizers or audience members, record parts of your presentation to use as promotional material, and share your success on social media or your website.

After my national conference session, I used the feedback and testimonials I received to secure more speaking opportunities. I also shared snippets of the presentation on LinkedIn, which attracted even more interest from potential clients and event organizers.

Exercise: After each speaking engagement, ask for feedback and testimonials from the event organizer or attendees. Use these testimonials to build credibility and promote your next speaking opportunities. Share highlights of your talk on your blog, social media, or website.

Public Speaking as a Pathway to Authority

Mastering public speaking isn't just about delivering information—it's about creating connection, building trust, and demonstrating your expertise in a way that leaves a lasting impact. The more you speak, the more people will see you as the go-to expert in your field. And each time you take the stage, whether in person or virtually, you'll be expanding your influence, growing your network, and solidifying your authority.

As you continue to build your speaking presence, remember that it's about progress, not perfection. Start small, refine your message, and with each opportunity, you'll become more confident, more impactful, and more recognized as a leader in your industry.

In the next chapter, we'll explore how to leverage **content creation**—another essential tool for expanding your reach and building your authority in your field.

Key Takeaway: Public speaking is one of the fastest ways to build authority and demonstrate expertise. By securing speaking engagements, crafting compelling presentations, and delivering your message with confidence, you can connect with your audience, expand your reach, and position yourself as a go-to expert in your field.

As you've seen, public speaking can be a powerful way to demonstrate your expertise and build credibility. But beyond live presentations, there's another essential tool that can help you maintain and grow your influence over time: **content creation**. Whether it's through blogs, videos, or social media posts, consistently sharing valuable content not only keeps you visible but also establishes you as a trusted expert. In the next chapter, I'll show you how creating content has elevated my own authority and how you can leverage it to do the same.

CHAPTER 8:
Leveraging Content Creation to Build Authority

Early on in my journey, I knew that in order to build lasting authority, I needed to stay visible and keep providing value to my audience. But I didn't always have the time to travel for speaking engagements or lead workshops. That's when I realized the power of **content creation**. Through blogging, creating videos, and sharing insights on social media, I could reach my audience consistently, no matter where I was or what my schedule looked like.

One of my first successes came from my blog. I started writing articles on topics related to course design, instructional storytelling, and entrepreneurship. At first, my posts were aimed at answering common questions I heard from clients and colleagues. But over time, something incredible happened—my blog posts began to attract more and more readers, not just from my local network but from people across the globe. As I shared practical tips, case studies, and personal experiences, I began to notice how this content was establishing me as a trusted voice in my field.

The same thing happened when I started posting video tutorials on YouTube and sharing insights on social media. By regularly creating and sharing content, I wasn't just putting my name out there—I was building relationships. My audience saw me as a consistent source of value, which made them more likely to follow my advice, trust my expertise, and, ultimately, become clients or collaborators.

Content creation became one of the most effective ways to grow my authority. It allowed me to showcase my knowledge, engage with my audience, and stay top-of-mind, even when I wasn't physically present at an event or in a meeting. And the best part? The more valuable content I shared, the more opportunities it generated—new speaking engagements, client inquiries, partnerships, and more.

Why Content Creation is Key to Staying Relevant and Building Authority

In today's digital world, content creation is one of the most powerful tools at your disposal for building and maintaining your authority. It's how you keep your audience engaged and remind them of the value you offer. Without regular content, even the most experienced experts risk fading from view. Consistently sharing high-quality, actionable content keeps you **relevant**, **visible**, and **trustworthy**.

Here's why content creation is essential:

- **Visibility:** Regular content keeps you top-of-mind for your audience. When they see your name attached to valuable insights, they're reminded of your expertise.

- **Trust:** Creating helpful content builds trust. When your audience learns from you, they see you as a reliable source of information and are more likely to follow your recommendations.

- **Connection:** Content allows you to stay connected with your audience. Whether through comments, shares, or direct messages, it opens the door to deeper engagement.

- **Authority:** Each piece of content you create showcases your knowledge. Over time, this adds up to a body of work that reinforces your authority in your field.

Building a Sustainable Content Creation Strategy

The key to leveraging content creation is to build a strategy that's **sustainable** and **aligned** with your expertise. You don't need to be everywhere or create every type of content. The goal is to find the formats that work best for you and your audience, and to deliver value consistently.

Here's how to develop a content creation strategy that elevates your authority:

1. Choose Your Formats

There are many different content formats to choose from—blogs, podcasts, videos, social media posts, and more. The key is to focus on the formats that best suit your strengths and the way your audience prefers to consume content.

For me, writing comes naturally, so blogging has always

been a central part of my content strategy. However, I also discovered that video tutorials on platforms like YouTube allowed me to reach a broader audience, especially when it came to demonstrating complex ideas in a visual way.

Exercise: Identify the content formats that play to your strengths. Are you a strong writer? Consider blogging or writing articles on LinkedIn. Do you enjoy speaking and teaching? Video content or podcasts might be your ideal format. Start with one or two formats that feel manageable and build from there.

2. Define Your Core Topics

To create content that builds your authority, you need to focus on the topics where your expertise shines. What are the key areas of your field where you can provide the most value? What questions does your audience consistently ask? These are the topics that should form the foundation of your content strategy.

For example, my core topics include course creation, instructional design, and storytelling for business. By focusing on these areas, I've been able to establish myself as an expert in a specific niche, which has helped me attract a targeted, engaged audience.

Exercise: Make a list of 3-5 core topics that align with your zone of genius. These are the subjects you'll regularly create content around. Stay focused on these areas to build your reputation as an authority in your field.

3. Create a Content Calendar

Consistency is key when it comes to content creation. One of the best ways to stay consistent is to create a **content calendar**. This helps you plan ahead, stay organized, and ensure you're delivering value to your audience on a regular basis.

For my own content strategy, I plan my blog posts, videos, and social media updates a month in advance. I decide which topics to cover, when to publish them, and how I'll promote them. This way, I can focus on creating quality content without the stress of last-minute scrambling.

Exercise: Create a simple content calendar for the next month. Decide how often you'll publish content and what topics you'll cover. Whether it's one blog post per week or a video tutorial every month, setting a schedule will help you stay consistent.

4. Repurpose Content Across Platforms

One of the most efficient ways to create content without burning out is to **repurpose** what you've already created. For example, a blog post can be turned into a series of social media posts, a podcast episode, or even a short video. Repurposing allows you to reach different audiences without constantly creating new material from scratch.

I often repurpose my blog posts into video scripts or take key points from a longer article and turn them into bite-sized tips for Instagram. This allows me to share my message across multiple platforms while staying efficient with my time.

Exercise: Look at your existing content and brainstorm ways to repurpose it. Could a popular blog post become a YouTube tutorial? Could you expand on a social media post in a podcast episode? Repurposing helps you maximize the impact of every piece of content.

5. Engage with Your Audience

Content creation isn't just about broadcasting your expertise—it's about creating a dialogue with your audience. Respond to comments, ask for feedback, and encourage discussion. This engagement builds deeper connections and helps you refine your content based on what resonates most with your followers.

I make it a point to reply to comments on my blog posts and YouTube videos, and I often ask my audience what topics they'd like to see me cover next. This not only keeps the conversation going but also ensures that my content is aligned with their needs.

Exercise: After publishing your next piece of content, engage with your audience by responding to comments or starting a conversation around the topic. Ask questions that invite participation, and pay attention to what resonates with your readers or viewers.

The Long-Term Impact of Consistent Content Creation

By consistently creating and sharing content, you're building a **body of work** that reinforces your authority over time. Each piece of content adds to your credibility, helps you reach new audiences, and keeps you visible in a crowded marketplace. Over time, your content becomes a powerful tool for attracting opportunities, whether that's new clients, speaking engagements, or collaborations.

As you develop your content creation strategy, remember

that the goal is **sustainability**. You don't need to do everything all at once. Start small, stay consistent, and focus on delivering value through the formats and topics that best showcase your expertise.

In the next chapter, we'll explore how to stay relevant as an expert in a rapidly changing world and the importance of continuous learning to maintain your authority.

Key Takeaway: Consistently creating and sharing high-quality content is essential for building and maintaining authority. By choosing the right formats, focusing on core topics, and engaging with your audience, you can establish a sustainable content creation strategy that showcases your expertise and keeps you relevant in your field.

As your content continues to establish your authority and deepen your connection with your audience, it's important to recognize that expertise is never static. Industries shift, new technologies emerge, and what worked yesterday might not work tomorrow. Staying relevant means continuously evolving, learning, and adapting to these changes. In the next chapter, I'll share how I've navigated the rapid changes in the e-learning industry and offer strategies to help you remain at the forefront of your field.

CHAPTER 9:
Evolving as an Expert—Staying Relevant in a Changing World

When I first started in e-learning and instructional design, the landscape was very different from what it is today. Back then, courses were primarily text-based, and tools like PowerPoint and Adobe Captivate were the industry standard. Over the years, however, the rise of interactive content, video-based learning, and AI-driven platforms completely transformed the field. If I had stayed with the same strategies I was using a decade ago, my work would have quickly become outdated.

Instead of resisting these changes, I made it a priority to **evolve**. I invested time in learning new technologies, from Articulate 360 to AI tools, and I adapted my content strategies to incorporate video, interactive modules, and more engaging formats. I also kept a close eye on emerging trends, like microlearning and gamification, which are now critical components of many e-learning programs.

One of the most pivotal shifts came when I began to

incorporate **AI-driven learning platforms** into my course design. This technology allowed for more personalized learning experiences, which greatly improved user engagement and outcomes. As I embraced these new tools and ideas, I not only kept my own work relevant but also continued to position myself as a leader in the e-learning space.

The ability to **evolve** is what keeps you at the forefront of your industry. Whether it's adopting new technologies, shifting your approach based on audience feedback, or keeping up with industry trends, evolution is a constant part of remaining an expert.

Why Ongoing Learning is Crucial for Maintaining Authority

In any field, there's a risk of becoming obsolete if you stop learning. The world moves quickly, and industries evolve faster than ever before. What worked last year may no longer be effective today, and new tools or trends can reshape your industry almost overnight.

As an expert, your ability to adapt is one of the most valuable skills you can cultivate. By staying current, you:

- **Maintain Relevance:** When you adapt to new trends and technologies, you stay relevant to your audience and your industry. Your expertise continues to meet the needs of the moment, rather than becoming outdated.

- **Deepen Your Authority:** Continuous learning allows you to expand your knowledge and offer new, cutting-edge solutions. This not only strengthens your authority but also positions you as someone who leads, rather than follows, industry trends.

- **Build Confidence:** The more you learn, the more confident you become in navigating change. This confidence translates into your work, helping you innovate and take on new challenges with ease.

Strategies for Staying Relevant in Your Field

To remain an authority and continue delivering value, you need a proactive approach to learning and adapting. Here are some strategies to help you evolve as an expert and stay ahead of the curve:

1. Stay Informed About Industry Trends

One of the best ways to stay relevant is by regularly following industry trends. Subscribe to newsletters, read industry publications, and follow thought leaders in your field. Pay attention to the latest tools, strategies, and innovations that are shaping your industry.

For me, staying informed about developments in e-learning—like the rise of AI, gamification, and immersive learning—helped me anticipate changes and adapt my offerings accordingly. This kept my content fresh and aligned with what my audience needed.

Exercise: Identify a few key sources of industry news—blogs, podcasts, or newsletters—that you can follow to stay updated. Set aside time each week to review the latest trends and think about how they apply to your work.

2. Invest in Professional Development

Ongoing learning requires investment—not just of time, but sometimes money. Attending workshops, webinars, and conferences is a great way to stay at the forefront of your field. You can also take online courses to learn new skills or deepen your expertise in areas where you want to grow.

I've attended numerous e-learning conferences and workshops over the years, and each one has provided me with valuable insights into emerging trends and technologies. These events also allowed me to network with other experts and stay connected to the broader industry community.

Exercise: Create a professional development plan for the next six months. What skills do you want to improve? What new tools or technologies would you like to learn? Identify relevant courses, conferences, or workshops, and set goals for your continued learning.

3. Engage in Continuous Reflection and Feedback

One of the most powerful ways to stay relevant is by continuously reflecting on your work and seeking feedback from your audience. What's working well? What can be improved? Are there emerging needs or challenges that you haven't yet addressed? Regular reflection helps you adapt and evolve based on real-world insights.

In my own work, I regularly ask my clients and course participants for feedback. Their insights help me refine my content, update outdated methods, and incorporate new tools that improve learning outcomes. This cycle of reflection and improvement is crucial for staying relevant.

Exercise: Set up a regular feedback loop with your audience. Whether it's through surveys, comments, or direct conversations, seek feedback on your products, services, or content. Use this feedback to identify areas for improvement or innovation.

4. Experiment with New Tools and Technologies

One of the best ways to stay ahead of the curve is by experimenting with new tools and technologies. Whether it's incorporating AI into your workflows, trying out new content platforms, or using data analytics to better understand your audience, being open to experimentation can keep your expertise fresh and relevant.

For example, when I first started using AI tools to create personalized learning experiences, it was an experiment. But as I saw the positive impact it had on engagement and retention, I integrated AI into more of my projects, which positioned me as a forward-thinking expert in my field.

Exercise: Identify one new tool or technology that's emerging in your industry. Commit to experimenting with it, either through a small project or by integrating it into your current work. Track the results and see how it enhances your offerings.

5. Cultivate a Growth Mindset

Ultimately, staying relevant requires a **growth mindset**—the belief that you can always learn, grow, and adapt. Embrace the challenges that come with new developments and see them as opportunities to expand your expertise. The experts who thrive are the ones who are curious, flexible, and always willing to push the boundaries of their knowledge.

In my career, I've always embraced the idea that there's

more to learn. Whether it's a new technology, a different approach to course design, or even feedback that challenges my current methods, I view every new development as an opportunity to grow. This mindset has kept me resilient in the face of change and allowed me to continuously evolve.

Exercise: Reflect on your own mindset when it comes to learning and adapting. Do you embrace change, or do you resist it? What steps can you take to cultivate a more proactive approach to learning and growth?

The Long-Term Benefits of Continuous Learning

When you commit to evolving as an expert, the benefits go far beyond staying relevant. You open yourself up to new opportunities, deepen your impact, and continue to grow your authority in ways that keep you ahead of the curve. Here's how continuous learning can transform your career:

- **Expanded Expertise:** By learning new skills and exploring emerging trends, you expand the range of solutions you can offer to your clients or audience.

- **Increased Innovation:** Continuous learning fosters creativity and innovation, allowing you to develop new products, services, or strategies that set you apart from the competition.

- **Sustained Authority:** When you stay ahead of industry changes, your audience will continue to look to you as a trusted expert, knowing that you're always up-to-date on the latest developments.

As we move into the final chapter, we'll explore how to monetize your expertise in sustainable, scalable ways that ensure your authority continues to grow alongside your impact.

Key Takeaway: Expertise is not static. To remain an authority, you must continuously learn, adapt to new trends, and stay ahead of changes in your field. By investing in ongoing learning, experimenting with new tools, and cultivating a growth mindset, you ensure that your expertise stays relevant, impactful, and forward-thinking.

As we've explored, staying relevant and continuously evolving as an expert is crucial for maintaining your authority. But once you've built that authority, the next step is learning how to turn it into a sustainable, profitable business. Authority is powerful not just because it establishes you as a trusted expert, but because it opens doors to new revenue streams. In this final chapter, I'll share how I diversified my income through courses, coaching, and consulting, and provide you with a roadmap to do the same.

CHAPTER 10:
MONETIZING YOUR AUTHORITY FOR LONG-TERM SUCCESS

When I first established myself as an authority in course design and content creation, I was primarily offering consulting services. At that point, most of my income came from one-on-one client work, which was rewarding but also limiting. I realized that if I wanted to grow my business—and my impact—I needed to **diversify** my income streams.

The shift started with my **online courses**. I had already been helping clients package their expertise into courses, so I decided to do the same for myself. I created a series of courses on storytelling, instructional design, and building online learning experiences. These courses allowed me to serve a much larger audience than I ever could through one-on-one consulting. Not only did this scale my business, but it also helped me reach people who couldn't afford premium consulting services.

Next, I expanded into **group coaching**. Instead of only working with clients individually, I began offering coaching programs where I could guide small groups through the process of developing their own expertise and creating educational products. The beauty of group coaching is that it allows you to provide high-value guidance while maximizing your time and reach.

Finally, I added **high-level consulting** for organizations and professionals who wanted a more tailored approach. By offering premium consulting packages, I was able to work with fewer clients at a higher price point, which gave me the flexibility to focus on my other revenue streams as well.

These different income streams—courses, coaching, and consulting—allowed me to build a **sustainable, profitable business** that wasn't reliant on any one source of income. This diversification not only increased my revenue but also gave me the freedom to focus on the areas I was most passionate about.

Why Monetizing Your Authority Is Essential for Long-Term Success

Once you've built authority in your field, monetizing that authority allows you to achieve **financial stability** and **freedom**. It's not just about making money; it's about creating a business model that supports your goals and allows you to expand your reach. By offering different products and services that cater to varying levels of your audience's needs, you can ensure long-term success and scalability.

Here's why monetizing your authority is so important:

- **Financial Stability:** Diversifying your income streams ensures that your business remains profitable, even if one revenue stream slows down.

- **Scalability:** Products like courses and digital products allow you to scale your business, reaching a larger audience without increasing your workload.
- **Flexibility:** When you have multiple income streams, you can choose how you spend your time—whether it's working one-on-one with premium clients or focusing on passive income through digital products.

Blueprint for Turning Your Authority into a Profitable Business

Monetizing your authority requires a strategic approach. You'll need to think about your audience's needs, how to structure your offerings, and how to create a business model that aligns with your goals. Here's a blueprint for turning your expertise into a profitable business:

1. Create High-Value Digital Products

One of the most scalable ways to monetize your authority is by creating **digital products**. These can include online courses, eBooks, templates, or membership programs that allow your audience to access your expertise without you being directly involved in every transaction.

Online courses are particularly powerful because they allow you to package your knowledge into a structured learning experience that can be sold to hundreds or even thousands of people. Once you've created the course, it can generate passive income for years.

For example, my first course on instructional storytelling became a cornerstone of my business. By automating the sales process through webinars and email marketing, I was able to sell the course while focusing on other areas of my business.

Exercise: Identify a topic or skill from your expertise that could be turned into a digital product. Outline the structure for an online course, eBook, or toolkit that would provide value to your audience. Start small—your first digital product doesn't have to be perfect; it just needs to offer actionable insights that solve a specific problem.

2. Offer Premium Coaching and Consulting

While digital products provide scalability, **premium coaching** and **consulting** allow you to offer high-value, personalized services to clients who need more tailored support. These higher-ticket services can significantly increase your income without requiring a large volume of clients.

For me, premium consulting became an important part of my business once my reputation as an authority was well-established. Organizations were willing to pay more for my services because they knew I could deliver results. This allowed me to raise my rates and choose projects that aligned with my expertise and interests.

Exercise: Develop a premium coaching or consulting package that provides in-depth, personalized guidance. Clearly define what's included—whether it's one-on-one sessions, group coaching, or a full consulting engagement—and set pricing that reflects the value you bring as an expert.

3. Build a Membership or Subscription Program

If you have a loyal audience, consider offering a **membership program** or subscription-based service that provides ongoing value. Membership programs often include exclusive content, live Q&A sessions, group coaching, or other perks that keep members engaged and learning over time.

This model provides recurring income and helps deepen your relationship with your audience. A membership program is also a great way to build a community around your expertise, which we discussed in Chapter 6.

Exercise: Outline what your membership program would offer. What ongoing content or value can you provide that encourages people to subscribe month after month? Think about what exclusive access or support your audience would find valuable.

4. Leverage Speaking and Workshops for Additional Revenue

As we explored in Chapter 7, public speaking is a powerful way to build authority—but it can also be a lucrative revenue stream. Once you've established yourself as an expert, you can monetize your speaking engagements by charging for workshops, keynotes, or seminars.

Speaking engagements not only pay well but also position you as a leader in your field, opening up even more opportunities for clients, partnerships, and media appearances.

Exercise: Create a speaking package that includes your key topics and services. Reach out to event organizers, businesses, or conferences that align with your expertise, and offer to lead a workshop or deliver a keynote presentation.

5. Maximize Your Reach Through Affiliate Marketing or Partnerships

Another way to monetize your authority is through **affiliate marketing** or **strategic partnerships**. If you use or recommend products, services, or tools in your field, you can partner with companies to earn a commission for promoting their offerings. This works particularly well if you've built a strong following that trusts your recommendations.

For example, if you regularly recommend software or tools that are essential to your audience's success, you can become an affiliate and earn passive income each time someone purchases through your referral.

Exercise: Identify companies or products that align with your expertise and audience. Reach out to see if they offer affiliate programs, or explore partnerships where you can provide exclusive deals or bonuses for your audience.

Long-Term Success Through Diversification

Monetizing your authority doesn't mean relying on one income stream. The most successful experts diversify their offerings, creating a business model that's scalable, sustainable, and adaptable to different audiences. Whether you're selling digital products, offering premium coaching, or speaking at events, each income stream reinforces your authority and creates opportunities for growth.

The key is to focus on building **long-term value**. Each product, service, or partnership you create should align with your overall goals and the needs of your audience. By doing this, you'll not only monetize your expertise but also ensure that your business continues to thrive and evolve.

As we conclude this journey together, remember that building authority is just the beginning. The real success comes when you learn how to turn that authority into a thriving, profitable business that grows alongside your influence.

Key Takeaway: Once you've established yourself as an expert, you can monetize your authority by offering a variety of products and services—from digital products to premium coaching and speaking engagements. By diversifying your income streams, you create a sustainable, profitable business that supports long-term success and growth.

Throughout this journey, we've explored how to build authority, package your expertise, and turn your knowledge into a thriving business. But the true power of authority goes beyond just professional success—it's about creating a lasting impact. I've seen firsthand how embracing your role as an authority can transform not only your career but also your life. In this final chapter, we'll reflect on that transformation and how you, too, can create a legacy of expertise.

CONCLUSION:
Creating Your Legacy of Expertise

One of the most rewarding experiences I've had as a coach was working with Maya, an educator with a passion for helping struggling students develop strong study habits. When Maya first came to me, she had years of knowledge but no clear path for how to scale her impact. She wanted to help more students and parents, but she wasn't sure how to position herself as an authority in the educational space.

We worked together to define her zone of genius and package her expertise into digital products, courses, and coaching programs. Over time, Maya became a sought-after speaker at education conferences, built a thriving online course, and developed a community of parents and educators who relied on her guidance. But the transformation didn't stop with her business. By stepping into her role as an authority, Maya not only grew her influence, but she also gained the confidence and fulfillment she had always sought. The real power of becoming an authority is that it changes how others see you—and more importantly, how you see yourself.

This is the essence of the "Meek Effect" that I've seen time and again with my clients. When you embrace your role as an expert, you unlock opportunities, build deeper connections, and, most importantly, create a **legacy** of impact. You become more than just a professional—you become a leader in your field.

Anyone Can Become an Authority

The journey to becoming an authority doesn't require extraordinary resources or opportunities. What it does require is the **right mindset, tools, and persistence**. If you're willing to invest in yourself—by refining your expertise, building your brand, and sharing your knowledge—you can position yourself as the go-to expert in your field.

It's important to remember that authority is not about being perfect or having all the answers. It's about being **consistent**, **authentic**, and **willing to serve**. Authority grows over time, and with every piece of content you share, every client you help, and every product you create, you build a foundation that supports your long-term success.

Take the First Steps Toward Your Authority

As you close this book, think about where you are right now and where you want to be. Maybe you're at the beginning of your journey, unsure of how to start. Maybe you've built a foundation but want to scale your impact. Wherever you are, the key is to **start taking action**. Authority isn't built in a day, but every small step you take moves you closer to becoming the expert people turn to in your industry.

So, what are the first steps you can take today?

- **Define your niche.** What is your zone of genius? Get

clear on the unique value you bring to the table.

- **Build your brand.** Craft a personal brand that reflects your expertise and resonates with your audience.

- **Share your knowledge.** Start creating content—whether it's a blog, podcast, or social media posts—that demonstrates your authority.

- **Package your expertise.** Turn your knowledge into products and services that allow you to scale your impact and grow your business.

No matter how small the first step, take it with confidence. The path to authority is a process, but every action you take brings you closer to creating a lasting legacy.

Believe in Your Impact

Never stop believing in the **impact** you can create. You have knowledge and experiences that are valuable to others, and by sharing them, you're making a difference in people's lives. Whether it's through helping clients solve problems, inspiring others to follow their dreams, or creating products that offer lasting value, your expertise has the power to transform lives.

Building authority is more than just a career move—it's a way to create **lasting influence**. The legacy you build today will continue to shape the lives of those you touch long into the future. So step confidently into your role as an authority, knowing that your voice, your expertise, and your story are needed.

Call to Action: Your journey to becoming an authority begins now. Take the lessons you've learned in this book and start applying them to your own life and career. Whether it's creating your first product, booking a speaking engagement, or building your community, every action you take moves you closer to your goal. Don't wait for the perfect moment—start today, and never stop believing in the **impact** you can create.

Your legacy of expertise is waiting to be built. The world needs what you have to offer—now go share it.

BOOKS IN THIS SERIES:
The Course Creator's Toolkit

The Course Creator's Toolkit series is designed for course creators who want to craft engaging, high-value courses that stand out in the crowded online education market. Based on real-world challenges faced by my clients, these books offer practical, step-by-step solutions to common pitfalls like low engagement, weak course design, or unclear outcomes.

Each chapter in the series feels like a personal coaching session with me, Meek Dual. I am passionate about helping others package their expertise into courses that not only sell but transform lives. You'll learn how to create interactive learning experiences, market your courses effectively, and build communities that keep learners engaged.

If you're ready to avoid the mistakes that hold most course creators back and build a profitable, high-perceived value course, this series is your blueprint for success.

Book 1: The Authority Advantage: Build Your Influence, Impact, and Income by Sharing What You Know

Are you ready to transform your expertise into influence, impact, and income?

In The Authority Advantage, entrepreneur and success coach Meek Dual reveals the proven strategies to help you become the go-to expert in your field. Whether you're an entrepreneur, coach, consultant, or creative professional, this book is your step-by-step guide to building lasting authority by leveraging the skills and knowledge you already possess.

Drawing from her own experiences and the journeys of countless successful clients, Meek shows you exactly how to:

- Find Your Zone of Genius: Identify the unique strengths that set you apart from the competition.

- Build a Personal Brand: Craft a brand that resonates with your ideal audience and communicates your value.

- Package Your Expertise: Turn your knowledge into profitable products and services, from online courses to consulting packages.

- Expand Your Influence: Use content creation and public speaking to grow your authority and reach more people.

- Stay Relevant: Learn how to continuously evolve as an expert and adapt to industry trends.

This book is packed with practical exercises, real-life case studies, and actionable steps that will help you create a legacy of influence while generating new income streams. You don't have to be a celebrity or a seasoned speaker to build authority. With the right mindset, tools, and persistence, anyone can become the expert others turn to for guidance and solutions.

Ready to amplify your authority and take your business to the next level?

Whether you're just starting out or you're ready to scale your impact, The Authority Advantage will give you the roadmap to success.

Get your copy today and start building the influence, impact, and income you deserve!

Book 2: Course Creator's Gold: Build Interactive Courses that Stick and SELL

Are you ready to transform your expertise into an engaging, high-value online course that captivates learners and generates revenue?

Course Creator's Gold is your step-by-step guide to creating courses that not only teach but inspire real transformation.

Packed with practical strategies and insights from my years of experience helping clients overcome the common pitfalls of course creation, this book is like having a personal coaching session with me, Meek Dual. I've helped countless women course creators who struggled with flat, disengaging content, unclear goals, and low sales. Now, I'm sharing the proven techniques that can help you avoid these challenges and build a course that not only sells but creates lasting impact.

Inside Course Creator's Gold, you'll learn:

- How to design interactive and dynamic learning experiences that keep your students engaged.

- Proven methods for crafting clear, actionable course goals that motivate learners.

- Practical tips for marketing your course and positioning it as a must-have solution in a crowded market.

- Strategies for building a supportive community around your course that fosters long-term engagement.

Whether you're just getting started or looking to refine your current course, Course Creator's Gold gives you the tools to create an online course that sells and delights learners. Start your journey toward course creation success today!

Book 3: Followers to Friends: Build Authentic Connections and Lasting Success Online

Ready to turn your followers into loyal, engaged supporters who trust and champion your brand?

In From Followers to Friends, success coach and creative visionary Meek Dual reveals the step-by-step strategies you need to build real, lasting connections online. Whether you're an entrepreneur, content creator, or professional seeking to grow your influence, this book is your roadmap to transforming followers into a true community—one rooted in trust and authenticity.

It's not about vanity metrics—it's about building trust. Through practical insights, real-life stories, and actionable steps, Meek shows you exactly how to:

- Build Trust: Learn why trust is the foundation of all online success and how to earn it through authenticity and consistency.

- Share Your Story: Craft an authentic digital persona that resonates deeply with your audience.

- Create Lasting Engagement: Develop strategies that encourage meaningful interactions and keep your audience coming back for more.

- Grow a Loyal Community: Move beyond just gaining followers and focus on building a supportive, engaged group of true fans.

- Handle Criticism with Grace: Turn negative feedback into opportunities for deeper connection and credibility.

With Meek's expert guidance, you'll learn how to build a sustainable online presence that doesn't just attract followers—it turns them into friends, loyal customers, and advocates for your brand. Packed with practical exercises and actionable advice, this book provides the tools you need to create real, lasting impact in the digital world.

Plus, as a bonus, you can access the FREE companion workbook to help you put these strategies into action and track your progress over the next 90 days.

Are you ready to transform your online presence and build a community that lasts?

Get your copy of From Followers to Friends today and start building the authentic connections that lead to lasting success!

ABOUT THE AUTHOR

Meek Dual is an entrepreneur, educator, and success coach with a passion for helping individuals unlock their true potential by sharing what they know. With years of experience in e-learning, course design, and content creation, Meek has built a thriving business by guiding professionals on how to package their expertise and position themselves as industry leaders. Her unique blend of storytelling, instructional design, and personal branding has earned her a reputation for transforming knowledge into influence, impact, and income.

As a single mother of children with learning challenges, Meek knows firsthand the challenges of balancing multiple roles while pursuing personal and professional growth. Her journey has been defined by resilience, determination, and the belief that everyone has the ability to become an authority in their field. This philosophy has shaped her approach to coaching, where she helps others recognize their strengths and leverage them to build successful brands, businesses, and legacies.

In her coaching programs and courses, Meek has empowered countless entrepreneurs, educators, and creatives to embrace their expertise and build profitable, scalable businesses. She is known for her practical, no-nonsense advice combined with a deep sense of empathy and encouragement for her clients' unique journeys.

When she's not coaching or designing courses, Meek is a sought-after speaker at conferences and workshops, sharing her insights on personal branding, content creation, and building authority. Her ability to connect with diverse audiences and deliver actionable strategies has made her a respected voice in the entrepreneurial space.

The Authority Advantage, Meek's latest book, encapsulates her proven framework for building influence, impact, and income. Through this book, she aims to inspire a new generation of women entrepreneurs to step into their power, share their expertise, and create lasting success.

To learn more about Meek and her work, visit MeekDual.com, where you'll find resources, coaching programs, and upcoming events designed to help you amplify your authority and achieve your dreams.

www.ingramcontent.com/pod-product-compliance
Lightning Source LLC
Chambersburg PA
CBHW050323230526
45471CB00005B/2318